Fermentation for Beginners

Delicious Fermented Vegetable Recipes for
Better Digestion and Health

Savannah Gibbs

The trademarks that are used are without any consent, and the publication of the trademark is without permission or backing by the trademark owner. All trademarks and brands within this book are for clarifying purposes only and are owned by the owners themselves, not affiliated with this document.

ISBN: 978-1-64842-091-7

Table of Contents

Chapter 1: Why Ferment Vegetables: Understanding Health Benefits 1

Why Ferment Vegetables: A History Lesson 1
Why Ferment Vegetables: Definitions 2
Why Ferment Vegetables: The Benefits 2

Chapter 2: How to Ferment Vegetables.................... 5

How to Ferment Vegetables: Salt... 5
How to Ferment Vegetables: Creating the Conditions 6
How to Ferment Vegetables: Equipment and Containers.... 7
How to Ferment Vegetables: Preparing and Storing the Food 7
How to Ferment Vegetables: Pitfalls.................................... 8

Chapter 3: How to Make Sauerkraut at Home 10

Ingredients Needed: 10
Process for how to make sauerkraut 11

Chapter 4: How to Make Fermented Pickles 13

How to Make Fermented Pickles: Ingredients 13
How to Make Fermented Pickles - Instructions 14

Chapter 5: How to Make Kimchi 15

How to Make Kimchi: Ingredients...................................... 15
How to Make Kimchi: Process 16

Chapter 6: How to Make Fermented Salsa 18

How to Make Fermented Salsa: Ingredients 18
How to Make Fermented Salsa: Process.............................. 19

Chapter 7: Recipes of Fermented Vegetables 20

Turkey Kielbasa and Sauerkraut..20
Pork Chops with Sauerkraut and Apples............................21
Italian Antipasto Platter...22
Black Bean Burgers 23
Pickle Slaw Burgers...24
Pickled Salmon..25
Tuna Salad...26
Breakfast Burrito...27
Tropical Chicken Bowl 28
Salsa Meatloaf 29
Cod with Lime and Salsa..30
Bean Soup with Fermented Salsa 31
Kimchi Vegetable Stew...32
Kimchi Fried Rice with Squid and Poached Egg 33
Spicy Kimchi and Chicken Noodles 35
Crockpot Sausage with Potatoes and Sauerkraut.............36
Grilled Steak with Cilantro Sauce and Fermented Radish. 37
Stir-Fry with Rice 38

Conclusion 39
Check Out My Other Books 41

Chapter 1: Why Ferment Vegetables: Understanding Health Benefits

Fermenting vegetables is a healthy way to eat and cook that doesn't put too much of a strain on your time, budget, or other resources. The necessary equipment is minimal and once you understand the process and the techniques, you'll find these foods can easily become a regular part of your diet. If you're wondering why ferment vegetables, the answer is pretty simple–better health from head to toe. Fermented vegetables contain things that are good for your stomach, digestion and even your brain. Understanding the history of this type of food preparation and the benefits that can be gained from it will help you embrace eating fermented foods, particularly fermented veggies.

Why Ferment Vegetables: A History Lesson

Fermentation was originally used as a way to preserve food. Ancient civilizations without the benefit of cold storage needed to keep the food they harvested for as long as possible. Anthropologists tell us that the first fermented foods that humans consumed were likely fruits. Once alcohol was discovered as a way to preserve food, bread making and fermentation really gained popularity. The first place that vegetables were fermented was probably China. They developed molds that were used to keep vegetables from rotting too soon to be enjoyed.

The process of fermenting food has undergone many changes throughout cultures and historical periods. However, it is something that has primarily been passed down from generation to generation and from older family members to younger. Cooking and food preparation is an important part of community and family bonds. So while there might not be history books written about food fermentation, it's a skill and a process that has been shared over the last hundreds and even thousands of years. It is traditional.

Why Ferment Vegetables: Definitions

If you don't have a lot of experience with fermentation, you might be wondering what it is, exactly. The Food and Agriculture Organization of the United Nations defines the process as a slow decomposition of organic materials of plant or animal origins. The decomposition is brought on by micro-organisms and enzymes. It doesn't mean that the food is going bad or turning rotten. It simply means that the substance of the food is changing, due to the fermentation process.

Vegetables are low in acid, unlike fruits. This can create a situation where the veggies are more likely to deteriorate before they can be eaten or processed, so fermentation helps them stick around a little longer. Fermenting vegetables requires the enzymes and micro-organisms to raise the level of acidity in the food, and that's done by pickling, salting, or drying them out. Natural bacteria are put to work and they increase the amount of lactic acid while breaking down the sugar and starch in vegetables.

Why Ferment Vegetables: The Benefits

Eating fermented vegetables can help with weight loss, better gut health, easier digestion, improved mood and an overall healthier physical and mental environment for your body and mind. One of the most important ingredients in fermented vegetables are probiotics. These probiotics plant beneficial bacteria into the digestive system and keep everything balanced internally.

A healthy ecosystem of probiotics in your gut can prevent and possibly reverse the onset of chronic diseases and other ailments. Probiotics will help your body store the things it needs and flush out the things it doesn't. They assist in building stronger immunity, which will keep you healthier overall. You'll also benefit from better bowel health, improved digestion, and a clean, clear intestinal tract. Many recent studies have called the gut a "second brain," meaning it needs just as much care and attention as the brain in your head. Probiotics that come from fermented vegetables can help.

When you eat fermented vegetables, you also do a better job of absorbing the vitamins and minerals you need. The digestive enzymes in those fermented foods will go to work and help you absorb the necessary nutrients that keep you in good shape.

A body that is better balanced will function better. If you're trying to lose weight, you know you need to eat more vegetables and less starchy foods and sugar-filled products. Fresh veggies are great, and fermented veggies can also help you flush out excess water and toxins that you might be holding on to. Eating this way will improve your chances of slimming down and help you learn to eat better in general.

If you're still wondering why ferment vegetables, you need to taste them. They're delicious and healthy, they last longer than the fresh veggies you keep in your fridge, and the fermentation process is neither expensive nor time consuming. With just a little effort and a lot of ambition, you can be fermenting your own vegetables and reaping the many benefits that come with eating these foods. Your body and mind will be better balanced, less prone to disease and a lot happier.

Chapter 2: How to Ferment Vegetables

It's one thing to be on board with the health benefits of eating fermented vegetables. However, it's another thing completely to set about fermenting them on your own. Don't worry. If you're wondering how to ferment vegetables, it's completely manageable. You'll be surprised at how little is required. Fermenting at home can be healthy and fun. There are just a few specifics you need to get straight when you're learning how to ferment vegetables yourself.

Most people find that fermented vegetables have a taste that is tangy or sour. Think of pickles or sauerkraut. That taste comes from the ability of lactic acid to break down sugar and starch in the vegetables. That's what you're trying to achieve.

How to Ferment Vegetables: Salt

Salt is a necessary ingredient when you're fermenting your own veggies. Salt helps to create the environment that's just right for fermentation. It allows micro-organisms to develop and grow. It protects your vegetables against the development of harmful bacteria while allowing the healthy bacteria to thrive.

You can use salt in a couple of different ways when you're fermenting your food. Simply tossing your vegetables in a good quantity of salt will draw water out of the veggies, preparing them to ferment properly. Use at least one tablespoon of salt for every pound of vegetables you want to ferment. You can also create a brine, which combines salt with water. In this process, the vegetables are soaked in the liquid before they ferment. Salt creates a stable and productive environment for your food.

How to Ferment Vegetables: Creating the Conditions

Food safety needs to be your primary concern when you're fermenting your own vegetables. Make sure you are creating the conditions that are safe, edible, and productive. If anything looks, smells, or tastes off–don't eat it. When you start with good, healthy vegetables that have not been exposed to bacteria such as E. coli or salmonella, you're in good shape. There are a few specific things to pay attention to as you are setting up your own fermenting system.

Temperature is important. Ideally, your fermentation process will take place between 60 degrees and 75 degrees. If you allow the temperature to slip below 60, the vegetables are unlikely to ferment at all. If the temperature goes higher than 75, the problem is that the food will become soft and too limp to enjoy. It might taste spoiled. If you're fermenting something such as sauerkraut, the ideal temperature is between 70 and 75 degrees. You'll have a fully fermented food product in just a few weeks.

When you reach the correct temperature of between 60 and 75 degrees, the harmful bacteria and potential pathogens will be destroyed by the healthy bacteria and the enzymes that you want to keep in your food. The right temperature will also keep the vegetables from rotting.

Many people who ferment their own food like to store the containers in a dark place or cover them with cloth to prevent light from affecting the food. The idea behind keeping the fermentation process dark is that you'll be able to preserve more of the Vitamin C in your vegetables this way. You never want to expose your vegetables to direct sunlight. Too much light will destroy the lactic bacteria, and that will corrupt your entire process. So, keep the fermenting vegetables in a dry, dark place that hovers between 60 degrees and 75 degrees.

You'll also need to keep your container in which you are fermenting free of oxygen. For example, if you're using a mason jar to ferment cucumbers or broccoli or cabbage, make sure the lid is on tight. There could be a build-up of gas a few days after fermentation starts, in which case you'll need to loosen the lid for a few seconds to allow the oxygen and carbon dioxide to escape. Lactic acid bacteria do not need oxygen to survive, and you don't want mold to develop.

How to Ferment Vegetables: Equipment and Containers

You have a few options when it comes to what you'll use to ferment your vegetables. There are specialty ceramic containers that are used to ferment foods, but any glass or plastic container that's high quality and sturdy will work. Make sure you don't use metal, because the acid will corrode it. You also don't want any dents, scratches or other anomalies to the container that will allow bad bacteria or other substances to creep in. A simple mason jar is one of the easiest containers to use. For basic fermentation, there is no special equipment to use or buy. As long as you have your container, everything can be done in your kitchen. There are elaborate vessels and crocks available, but purchasing those is not necessary.

How to Ferment Vegetables: Preparing and Storing the Food

Simply slice, chop, or cube the vegetables you want to ferment. You can use anything you like, such as onions, cucumbers, cabbage, broccoli, carrots, cauliflower, asparagus, and eggplant. The veggies should be clean and fresh and cut into uniform sizes that will fit into the container you've chosen. Depending on what you're fermenting and the recipe you're using, all you really have to do is cover the vegetables with water, sea salt and perhaps some herbs and spices.

You'll know the vegetables are fermenting because you'll see some bubbles begin to form. Tasting the veggies is the best way to determine whether the fermentation process is finished. They will keep fermenting even as they are stored. Start tasting them after a week and remember that the longer they ferment, the stronger the flavor will become. Store your vegetables in a cupboard or even in your refrigerator.

How to Ferment Vegetables: Pitfalls

Fermenting can often be a trial and error process. You might notice some mold, which means oxygen has crept in. The vegetables could taste terrible, in which case you need to adjust the length of time they ferment or the temperature at which they are stored. You might also notice that the brine you are fermenting your vegetables in begins to overflow or push against your lid. You'll need to release some of that pressure and possibly remove some vegetables if your container is too crowded.

If you notice a white foam developing on your vegetables, don't panic. If it's not fuzzy, then it's not mold. It could be yeast that is perfectly healthy. Keep it. What you don't want to see are insects. Remember that fermented food is live food. Some insects that were on the vegetables unbeknownst to you could have left some eggs on that food, and those eggs can hatch in the environment you've created. Compost that batch and start over.

Knowing how to ferment vegetables on your own can open up a new world of possibilities for you and your kitchen. It's not hard or frightening, and if you're willing to try it a few times, you will likely develop a system that works well and delivers delicious, healthy foods filled with probiotics and gut-gorgeous bacteria. Try the recipes in this book and don't be afraid to get creative on your own. Fermented vegetables can be enjoyed for weeks and even months.

Chapter 3: How to Make Sauerkraut at Home

One of the easiest fermentation projects to begin with is learning how to make sauerkraut. All you really need is cabbage and a mason jar. You might want to start making larger quantities of sauerkraut in the future, at which point it will be easier to use a crock for your fermenting process. However, learning to do it at home only requires a small batch, the perfect size for a mason jar.

Fermenting cabbage this way allows you to keep the vegetable longer than you would if you wanted to eat it raw or fresh. It also produces lactic acids and probiotics that are excellent for your health. Even more importantly, you'll love the taste.

Ingredients Needed:

1 head of green cabbage

1½ tablespoons of salt

1 sharp knife

1 mason jar with airtight lid

Process for how to make sauerkraut

1. Wash and dry the mason jar. For the good bacteria to take over any potential bad bacteria, a pristine environment is necessary.

2. Wash and dry the cabbage. Discard any limp or hanging outer leaves.

3. Keep one large leaf of cabbage to the side. Then, slice and chop the cabbage into thin strips. You ultimately want a pile of thin ribbons that are more or less uniform in size.

4. Put the cabbage into a large bowl and sprinkle the salt over it. After allowing it to rest for a couple of minutes, start massaging the salt into the cabbage by hand (make sure those hands are clean). Squeeze the cabbage as you work the salt into it. After about 10 minutes, you'll notice the cabbage is becoming wet and soft.

5. Pack the cabbage into the mason jar. Take one handful at a time and press the vegetables firmly into the bottom of the jar. Once you get to the top of your jar, take the leaf you set aside and place it over the shredded cabbage. This will keep the shredded pieces in place. It's very important for the cabbage to remain submerged in the liquid it produces in order for the fermentation process to work properly.

6. Tighten the lid over the jar and store it in a cool, dark, and dry location. Ideally, you'll find a spot with a temperature between 65 and 70 degrees.

7. Ferment the sauerkraut for three to five days. If you notice bubbles forming at the top of the jar, open the lid and allow the gas that's building up to escape.

8. Taste your sauerkraut. The longer you let it ferment, the stronger the taste will become. You can refrigerate it and the sauerkraut will keep for several months.

9. This is a simple explanation for how to make sauerkraut. You can get more creative and include red cabbage or add caraway seeds to the mixture for extra flavor while it ferments.

The basic sauerkraut recipe is a great way to begin fermenting vegetables. You'll enjoy the taste of your homemade sauerkraut, and it will build the confidence you need to continue fermenting more complex vegetables.

Chapter 4: How to Make Fermented Pickles

Pickles are delicious and instead of buying them at the store, you can create them in your own home. All you have to do is learn how to make fermented pickles, and it's not terribly complicated. When you ferment these vegetables to make pickles, you're harnessing the power of natural preservatives and acids. Once the process is complete, you can keep these pickles delicious and safe to eat for months in your refrigerator.

In order to create fermented pickles, you'll want to create a brine. Again; there are some fun and complex machines and equipment available to make your brining and your fermenting easier. However, you don't really need them. All you need for these pickles are the veggie you choose to use (cucumbers are highly recommended), salt, water and a clean glass or plastic jar with an air-tight lid. These instructions include dill and pepper to complement the taste of your pickles.

How to Make Fermented Pickles: Ingredients

1 half-gallon jar
1 sharp knife
2 pounds of small cucumbers
3 tablespoons sea salt
4 sprigs of fresh dill (or two tablespoons dried dill)
½ teaspoon black peppercorns

How to Make Fermented Pickles - Instructions

1. Clean and dry the jar and the cucumbers. Rinse the dill and set it aside.

2. Slice the cucumbers to desired thickness. You can slice them so they are round or slice them length-wise so they are long. This is up to you, just make sure they are cut in a length that will fit in your pickling jar.

3. Dissolve the salt in ¼ gallon of water. Stir it until you don't see the crystals anymore to create the brine.

5. Place the dill at the bottom of the jar and add the peppercorns. Pour the cucumber slices on top.

6. Pour the brine solution on top of the cucumbers. Secure the top of the jar with the lid. You can also use a clean cloth then put a fitted plate on top of the jar. Apply some weight to the plate so air doesn't get into the jar and cause mold.

7. Store the jar in a cool, dark place. The fermenting process will begin immediately and you'll have crispy sour pickles in a matter of days. The amount of time you need to fully ferment the pickles will be between two and four weeks, depending on the temperature. Keep the pickles for months in the fridge and enjoy them as snacks and sides.

This is how to make fermented pickles, and you can see it's not a difficult process. While the pickles are no longer raw cucumbers, they are in many ways even healthier for you than that raw vegetable form. You're getting beneficial cultures and awesome bacteria which are storming through your digestive tract and keeping your gut health in check.

These fermented pickles can be enjoyed right out of the jar, or you can toss them into salads. However you decide to eat them, you'll be glad you learned how to make your own instead of buying them.

Chapter 5: How to Make Kimchi

If you're not familiar with kimchi, it's a food you should get to know. This dish, primarily found in Korean cuisine, is made of fermented vegetables and spices. It's a traditional Asian food, and something you'll find both delicious, easy to make and excellent for your health. Most people eat it as a side dish and you can also use it in soups, stews, and salads.

How to Make Kimchi: Ingredients

Any combination of vegetables will work for your ingredients. These instructions will include some of the more traditional veggies used in kimchi, but you should feel free to experiment and use the foods you like best.

1 glass jar with tight lid
1 large bowl
1 small bowl
2 pounds napa cabbage
¼ cup sea salt
Some water
5 cloves garlic, minced
1 teaspoon ginger, minced
1 teaspoon sugar
4 tablespoons red pepper flakes
8 ounces radish, peeled and thinly sliced
4 scallions, cut into small pieces

How to Make Kimchi: Process

1. Wash the cabbage thoroughly under running water and pat dry. Using a sharp kitchen knife, cut into thin slices. Ensure you discard the cores.

2. Transfer the cabbage slices into a large bowl. Sprinkle sea salt over it. Using your hands, gently mix it all together. Make sure the cabbage is thoroughly coated with salt.

3. Add enough water to cover the cabbage. Cover it with a plate and place a heavy jar filled with water on top of the plate. This is done to weigh down the cabbage. Let this mixture stand for approximately 2 hours.

4. After a couple of hours, place the cabbage under running water and rinse 2-3 times. Drain the water and set the cabbage aside in a colander for about 20 minutes.

5. In a small bowl, combine the minced ginger, garlic, sugar and mix to form a smooth paste. Later, add the red pepper flakes and mix again.

6. Squeeze out the remaining liquid from the cabbage and place back in the same large bowl. Add the sliced radish, scallions, and seasoning from the small bowl and give it a good mix. Keep gently mixing for a few more minutes until all the ingredients are mixed well.

7. Fill a jar with the kimchi, pressing the vegetables down with your hands. Cover the jar and store your kimchi in a cool, dark place where the temperature will be no lower than 60 degrees and no higher than 75 degrees.

8. If you see bubbles float to the top of the jar, simply unscrew the lid and allow some of the gas to escape. Put the lid back on securely and allow it to continue fermenting.

9. After about a week, taste the kimchi. Once you get it to the desired balance of flavors, store it in the refrigerator and enjoy for several weeks.

Kimchi is an excellent addition to your supply of fermented foods. It tastes great with fish or steak, and it also makes a lovely base for a hot veggie soup. You can buy it already made in many stores, but when you know how to make kimchi on your own, it gives you a sense of accomplishment and pride. It also tastes better because you know exactly where the vegetables came from and how everything was prepared. Fermenting veggies into foods like kimchi is a great way to stay healthy and eating whole.

Chapter 6: How to Make Fermented Salsa

Tomatoes are, by nature, one of the healthiest foods you can eat. In their fresh, raw form, they are filled with vitamins, minerals and other ingredients packed with anti-oxidants to keep you healthy and fight off long term diseases like cancer and diabetes. Fermenting tomatoes will allow you to harness all that goodness and add some bonus health benefits. When you understand how to make fermented salsa, you get the combined veggies as well as probiotics that are present in fermented foods. The instructions here are for half a gallon of salsa. You'll find it's one of the tastiest salsas you've ever had, and you can enjoy it on chips, raw veggies or on top of meat, fish, and chicken.

How to Make Fermented Salsa: Ingredients

2 or 3 small glass canning jars with lids
2 pounds fresh tomatoes
1 red onion, chopped
1 red bell pepper, chopped
1 green bell pepper, chopped
1 orange bell pepper, chopped
5 garlic cloves, peeled
½ cup whole cilantro leaves
2 limes, juiced
3 tablespoons sea salt
½ teaspoon chili powder
½ cup whey

Everyone has differing tastes when it comes to salsa. If you like yours less spicy, cut down to 1/4 teaspoon of the chili powder. If you hate onion, leave it out. You can adjust these ingredients to what you prefer in your favorite tomato-based topping. The whey is present to help break down and ferment the tomatoes; if you're intolerant to whey, consider making a brine or using other already-fermented liquids.

How to Make Fermented Salsa: Process

1. Chop all the veggies into small pieces and combine in a bowl. Add the garlic and cilantro leaves. Add the lime juice, salt, chili powder and whey. Stir together and allow the mixture to settle for 30 minutes.

2. Clean and dry your containers or jars thoroughly. Everything has to be completely clean so you don't have mold or unhealthy bacteria growing on your salsa.

3. Spoon the salsa into the jars, close the lids tightly and leave the salsa to ferment at room temperature for three to five days, ideally between 65 degrees and 75 degrees.

4. You may notice the vegetables separate from the liquid, and there will also be bubbles forming at the top of the jars. Open the jars to press the veggies back into the liquid with a clean spoon. This will also allow the gas to escape. Reseal the lids and continue to ferment.

5. The salsa will be fully fermented after about a week, and if you keep it in your refrigerator, it will be edible for several months.

Once you know how to make fermented salsa, buying the premade jars at the grocery store will be impossible. Your fresh ingredients will ferment into something far more delicious, more economical, and easier to enjoy for longer. You might find it helpful to use a food processor to mince up all the veggies for you, especially if you prefer a less chunky salsa.

Chapter 7: Recipes of Fermented Vegetables

Now that you know how to ferment your own vegetables, you'll be looking for recipes that can incorporate those vegetables into meals. Try one of the recipes of fermented vegetables included below. You'll find that the fermented veggies you made yourself really complement the other food on your plate, and leave you feeling satisfied. They also taste great, and you know they're contributing to the healthy bacteria ecosystem in your digestive and intestinal tracts.

Turkey Kielbasa and Sauerkraut

Serves: 4
Ingredients:
1 pound turkey kielbasa
2 pints fermented sauerkraut
1 tablespoon caraway seeds
2 tablespoons olive oil
2 cups black beans, rinsed

Directions:
1. In a skillet, heat the olive oil. Poke fork holes into the kielbasa links and cook them in the oil over medium high heat until they brown on the outside, for about five minutes.

2. Remove the kielbasa and allow it to cool for three minutes. While it's cooling, add the sauerkraut and beans to the pan and stir in the caraway seeds.

3. Slice the kielbasa into one-inch pieces and return it to the pan.

4. Continue to cook all the ingredients together until the meat is cooked all the way through.

Pork Chops with Sauerkraut and Apples

Serves: 4
Ingredients:
4 pork chops, bone in
2 pints fermented sauerkraut
2 tablespoons olive oil
2 apples, peeled and sliced
1 tablespoon butter
1 tablespoon brown sugar
3 teaspoons dried rosemary
Salt and pepper

Directions:
1. Preheat the oven to 375 degrees F.

2. In a large skillet, heat the olive oil and add the pork chops. Sprinkle the salt, pepper and rosemary on the meat and cook until they are brown; 5 minutes on the first side and 3 minutes on the next.

3. Layer the bottom of a baking dish with the sauerkraut and place the pork chops on top. Cook in the oven for 30–40 minutes, until pork is done.

4. Meanwhile, in a small saucepan, melt the butter and stir in the brown sugar. Add the apple slices and toss.

Italian Antipasto Platter

Serves: 8
Ingredients:
2 cups fermented pickles
1 cup Kalamata olives
1 cups Spanish olives
1 cup fermented or pickled pearl onions
1 stick pepperoni, sliced
1 cup mozzarella cheese, cubed
1 stalks celery, chopped
1 cup marinated red peppers, sliced

Directions:
1. Toss all the ingredients together in a large bowl until all the food and flavors are blended. Serve in small bowls.
2. This recipe makes 8 servings as an appetizer.

Black Bean Burgers

Serves: 4
Ingredients:
4 black bean burger patties
1 cup fermented pickles
4 slices provolone cheese
4 tablespoons spicy mustard
½ cup red onion, sliced
Salt and pepper

Directions:
1. Heat a grill or a grill pan and cook the black bean burgers on each side until they are done.
2. Melt a slice of cheese on top of each burger before removing them from the heat.
3. Top with mustard, red onion, and fermented pickles.
4. If you want some bread, add a bun.
5. Season with salt and pepper.

Pickle Slaw Burgers

Serves: 6

Ingredients:

2 pounds fresh green cabbage

1 cup carrots, peeled and sliced

¾ cup mayonnaise

2 tablespoons white wine vinegar

4 tablespoons sugar

2 tablespoons dill pickle juice

½ teaspoon salt

½ cup dill pickles

½ teaspoon cayenne pepper

6 burger buns

Fresh cherries for garnishing

Directions:

1. Wash cabbage under running water and cut into thin slices.

2. Add cabbage to a large bowl. Combine with carrots, mayonnaise, white wine vinegar, salt, pepper, dill pickle juice, and dill pickles, and mix well with a spoon.

3. Refrigerate coleslaw for at least a couple of hours. Refrigerating it overnight will bring out more flavor.

4. Remove from fridge and mix well again.

5. Cut burger buns in half. Place coleslaw on each of the burger buns and secure with toothpick.

6. Garnish by adding fresh cherries on top.

Pickled Salmon

Serves: 4
Ingredients:
4 salmon fillets
1 tablespoon black peppercorns
3 tablespoons pickled cucumber
1 teaspoon dried thyme
Some fresh parsley
1 clove
2 tablespoons sweet paprika
4 tablespoons extra virgin olive oil
2 tablespoons apple cider vinegar
2 tablespoons white wine
Sea salt to taste

Directions:
1. Using a sharp kitchen knife, cut salmon into thin strips and spread on a large plate.
2. Season with salt, thyme leaves, peppercorns, clove, cucumber pickle, and paprika and mix well. Ensure salmon is fully coated with seasoning.
3. Heat 2 tablespoons of olive oil in a large skillet over medium heat.
4. Lay salmon pieces in pan and sprinkle with remaining 2 tablespoons olive oil.
5. Sprinkle with white wine vinegar.
6. Cover and cook salmon for about 10-11 minutes over low heat.
7. Garnish with fresh parsley leaves.
8. Salmon will keep in refrigerator for up to 2 days.

Tuna Salad

Serves: 4–6

Ingredients:

2 cans of tuna

½ cup fermented pickles

½ cup red bell pepper, diced

½ cup green bell pepper, diced

½ celery, diced

½ cup mayonnaise

1 tablespoon chopped parsley

1 tablespoon chopped thyme

1 tablespoon chopped rosemary

1 teaspoon sea salt

1 teaspoon white pepper

Crackers

Directions:

1. Combine all ingredients in a bowl except for pickles, and mix until combined.

2. Spread on crackers and top with pickles.

Breakfast Burrito

Serves: 4
Ingredients:
6 eggs
1 cup fermented salsa
1 tablespoon olive oil
1 tablespoon water
¼ cup red onion, diced
1 clove garlic, minced
½ cup bell pepper, diced
½ cup shredded cheddar cheese
½ cup sour cream
4 whole wheat tortillas
Salt and pepper

Directions:
1. Whisk the eggs with water, salt, and pepper.
2. In a skillet, cook the garlic, onion, and bell pepper in the olive oil.
3. Scramble the eggs in the skillet with the vegetables.
4. Cover the tortillas with shredded cheese.
5. Pour the egg mixture evenly into each tortilla. Top with sour cream and fermented salsa.

Tropical Chicken Bowl

Serves: 2

Ingredients:

1 cup brown rice

2 cups chopped chicken, cooked

½ cup red onion, chopped

1 cup black beans, cooked

1 cup yellow corn, cooked

1 cup fermented salsa

¼ cup sour cream

Directions:

1. Cook the brown rice according to your directions, and drain.

2. In a bowl, create layers of rice, beans, chicken, onion, corn, salsa, and sour cream.

Salsa Meatloaf

Serves: 10

Ingredients:
2 pounds ground turkey
1 cup fermented salsa
1 cup bread crumbs
1 large onion, chopped
3 minced garlic cloves
1 large egg
½ teaspoon salt
1½ cups chicken broth
½ teaspoon ground pepper

Directions:
1. In a bowl, combine salsa with chicken broth and bread crumbs, and mix well using a spoon. Set aside.
2. In another bowl, combine onions with minced garlic, ground turkey, and egg, and give it a mix.
3. Now, transfer the salsa mixture to this bowl and mix again.
4. Preheat the oven to 350 degrees F.
5. Take a loaf-shaped pan and grease it with some butter.
6. Pour the mixture into the pan and cover with foil.
7. Bake for about 60 minutes, until all the ingredients are cooked.
8. Let stand for a few moments to cool down.
9. Slice and serve.

Cod with Lime and Salsa

Serves: 4

Ingredients:

2 pounds fresh cod
1 tablespoon olive oil
2 limes
1 cup fermented salsa
Salt and pepper

Directions:

1. Preheat oven to 375 degrees F.

2. Slice limes and layer on the bottom of a baking dish.

3. Place the cod on top of the lime slices. Drizzle with olive oil, salt, and pepper. Cook for 20 minutes or until the fish turns flaky.

4. Remove from the oven and allow to cool for five minutes.

5. Spoon fermented salsa on top of fish.

6. This recipe pairs nicely with a salad or any crisp vegetable.

Bean Soup with Fermented Salsa

Serves: 4

Ingredients:
16 ounces black beans, soaked overnight
1 cup chicken broth
1 tablespoon olive oil
1 onion, chopped
1 teaspoon minced garlic cloves
16 ounces fermented salsa
2 tablespoons lime juice
2 teaspoons cumin powder
½ teaspoon salt
½ teaspoon paprika
2 tablespoons yogurt
Some freshly plucked cilantro leaves

Directions:

1. Boil some water in a saucepan. Add black beans and cover with a lid. Boil for about 15 minutes until the beans are thoroughly cooked. Remove from heat. Drain water and transfer beans to a food processor. Give it a whirl until it forms a paste. Set aside.

2. Heat the olive oil in a saucepan over medium-high heat.

3. Add minced garlic and onion and sauté for 2–3 minutes until it turns slightly brown.

4. Pour in the bean mixture, add salt, and cook for 3–4 minutes.

5. Add salsa, lime juice, chicken broth, cumin powder, and paprika and stir well using a large spoon. Bring the mixture to a boil.

6. Reduce heat and cook for another 20–25 minutes over low heat.

7. Garnish with chopped cilantro leaves, top it off with some yogurt and serve.

Kimchi Vegetable Stew

Serves: 4

Ingredients:
1 cup fermented kimchi
1 tablespoon olive oil
1 red onion, sliced
2 cups vegetable stock
1 teaspoon sugar
1 sweet potato, peeled and chopped into cubes
1 cup mushrooms, sliced
2 cups sliced cabbage
12 ounces tofu, sliced
¼ cup carrots, sliced

Directions:

1. Heat the olive oil in a large saucepan over medium heat and cook the onion, kimchi, and sugar for about 5 minutes.

2. Pour the vegetable stock into the pot as well as the sweet potato.

3. Cover the pot and simmer for about 15 minutes, until the sweet potato begins to soften.

4. Add cabbage, tofu, mushrooms, and carrots. Cook for an additional 10 minutes and serve with crusty bread.

Kimchi Fried Rice with Squid and Poached Egg

Serves: 4

Ingredients:

2 tablespoons canola oil

1 pound squid, cleaned and pieced

1 cup kimchi

¼ cup water

3 cups white rice, cooked

2 scallions, chopped

4 large eggs

1 tablespoons sesame oil

1 tablespoon toasted sesame seeds

½ teaspoon salt

Some ground pepper for garnishing as per taste

Directions:

1. Heat canola oil in a saucepan over medium heat.

2. Slide in the squid pieces and spread out in pan.

3. Sprinkle with salt and cook for about 60 seconds until browned. Once done, remove from flame and set aside in a bowl.

4. Heat sesame oil in the same pan over medium heat. Add kimchi, scallions, and water, and cook for 2-3 minutes.

5. Add rice and cook covered for about 7–8 minutes, until the liquid evaporates.

6. Add the squid back to the pan and cook for 1 minute.

7. Transfer this mixture into 4 separate bowls.

8. In the meantime, heat some water in a large saucepan until just before simmering. Do not to let it reach the point of simmering–keep the heat low.

9. Gently crack each egg into the saucepan and let cook for about 1 minute. Take poached eggs out using a flat spoon and place one on top of each bowl.

10. Season with pepper and serve.

Spicy Kimchi and Chicken Noodles

Serves: 4
Ingredients:
1 tablespoon bouillon
2 cups kimchi
3–4 tablespoons spicy garlic sauce
1 cup shitake mushrooms, sliced
4 ounces chicken leg pieces, sliced
3 cups ramen noodles
½ teaspoon salt
2 medium onions, thinly sliced
2 tablespoons salsa
2 tablespoons olive oil

Directions:
1. Boil some water in a large saucepan. Add noodles, cover with lid, and cook for 5–6 minutes. Once cooled, drain water and set aside.

2. Heat olive oil in a saucepan over medium heat.

3. Add garlic sauce and sliced onions and sauté for 2–3 minutes until the onions start to brown.

4. Throw in the shitake mushrooms and chicken pieces and cook for another 3–4 minutes. Add salsa, bouillon cube, salt, and mix well.

5. Gently slide the noodles into the saucepan and toss well with the chicken mixture. Cook for 2–3 minutes.

6. Serve hot.

Crockpot Sausage with Potatoes and Sauerkraut

Serves: 4

Ingredients:

1½ pounds potatoes

2 cups of sauerkraut

1 small onion, peeled and sliced

½ cup chicken broth

¼ cup white wine

1 teaspoon caraway seeds

Some freshly chopped parsley

1½ pounds bratwurst links

½ teaspoon salt

1 teaspoon olive oil

½ teaspoon pepper

Directions:

1. Wash the potatoes thoroughly and peel them. Dice using a sharp kitchen knife.

2. Heat the olive oil in a large pan over medium-high heat.

3. Add sliced onions and sauté for a couple of minutes until slightly brown.

4. Throw in the diced potatoes and sauerkraut and stir for 2 minutes.

5. Sprinkle salt, pepper, and caraway seeds and mix well using a spoon.

6. Add the bratwurst, chicken broth, and wine, and give it a stir again.

7. Transfer the mixture to your slow cooker. Cook the mixture for about 7–8 hours on low, or 5 hours on high.

8. Sprinkle chopped parsley leaves on top before serving.

Grilled Steak with Cilantro Sauce and Fermented Radish

Serves: 4

Ingredients:

½ cup fresh cilantro leaves, chopped

1 small jalapeno pepper, sliced

1 tablespoon red wine vinegar

3 tablespoons olive oil, divided

½ teaspoon kosher salt

½ teaspoon ground pepper

1 small onion, chopped

1 teaspoon ground cumin

1 cup frozen corn

1 cup fermented radish

½ cup heavy cream

1½ pounds steak, sliced

Directions:

1. In a bowl, combine jalapeno, chopped cilantro, red wine vinegar, 2 tablespoons of olive oil, salt, and pepper. Toss mixture well using a spoon.

2. Heat one tablespoon of olive oil in a saucepan over medium heat.

3. Add onion and sauté until tender. Throw in the corn kernels, salt, and ground pepper and stir-fry for about 4–5 minutes.

4. Pour the cream. Add ground cumin and cook for another 2 minutes or until mixture thickens.

5. Season steak with salt and pepper. Lay pieces in a large skillet and cook over medium heat for 5–6 minutes on both sides until slightly brown.

6. Transfer steak to a large plate. Add corn mixture on the side along with fermented radish and serve.

Stir-Fry with Rice

Serves: 4

Ingredients:

2 cups brown rice, cooked

1 pound lean skirt steak, cut into strips

1 cup red bell pepper, cut into strips

1 cup onions, cut into strips

1 cup carrots, shredded

1 cup Romano beans

1 tablespoon soy sauce

½ cup kimchi

1 tablespoon peanut oil

1 cup broccoli florets, chopped

Directions:

1. Heat the oil in a wok over medium high heat and add the steak, cooking for about 10 minutes.

2. Remove the meat and add the pepper, onions, carrots, beans, and broccoli to the wok.

3. Add the soy sauce and toss everything together, stirring until cooked.

4. Return the steak to the wok and add the kimchi. Stir all the ingredients together until heated and combined.

5. Place over a pile of rice, which should have been cooked according to package directions.

Conclusion

With the recipes of fermented vegetables in this book, you can get started on creating delicious, healthy, and satisfying recipes for your family, friends, or even just yourself. Having jars and containers of salsa, sauerkraut, kimchi, and pickles in the fridge will give you a lot of options any time you are looking for a creative way to cook a meal. In addition to tasting great, you'll be increasing your health benefits. The fermented foods you use will go to work in your gut, establishing an army of healthy bacteria ready to fight off potential diseases and chronic illnesses.

Finally, I want to thank you for reading my book. If you enjoyed the book, please take the time to share your thoughts and post a review on the book retailer's website. It would be greatly appreciated!

Best wishes,
Savannah Gibbs

Check Out My Other Books

Mediterranean Diet Cookbook: Easy and Delicious
Mediterranean Diet Recipes to Lose Weight and Lower Your
Risk of Heart Disease

Clean Eating Cookbook: Quick and Easy Clean Eating Recipes
to Lose Weight and Live Healthy

CPSIA information can be obtained
at www.ICGtesting.com
Printed in the USA
BVHW041154160221
600254BV00016B/242